T0191111

PRESENTED TO:

FROM:

DATE:

ENNEAGRAM TYPE

BETH McCORD
Your **Enneagram** Coach

THOMAS NELSON
Since 1798

Enneagram Type 2: The Supportive Advisor

© 2019 by Beth McCord

Published in Nashville, Tennessee, by Thomas Nelson. Thomas Nelson is a registered trademark of HarperCollins Christian Publishing, Inc.

Published in association with Alive Literary Agency.

Unless otherwise noted, Scripture quotations are taken from the ESV® Bible (The Holy Bible, English Standard Version®), copyright © 2001 by Crossway, a publishing ministry of Good News Publishers. Used by permission. All rights reserved.

Any Internet addresses, phone numbers, or company or product information printed in this book are offered as a resource and are not intended in any way to be or to imply an endorsement by Thomas Nelson, nor does Thomas Nelson vouch for the existence, content, or services of these sites, phone numbers, companies, or products beyond the life of this book.

Graphic Designer: Jane Butler, Well Refined Creative Director, wellrefined.co
Interior Designer: Emily Ghattas
Cover Designer: Greg Jackson at Thinkpen Design

ISBN-13: 978-1-4002-1569-0

Printed in China

21 22 23 24 25 GRI 10 9 8 7 6 5 4 3 2

Contents

Foreword

My son curled up with his special, most favorite monkey after a long summer day at the pool. He was sun-kissed and tired, his messy hair still damp from the bath. I tucked him into his crisp, cool sheets and ran my fingers through his hair. Like always, he rolled over to his belly as JJ Heller's rendition of "Over the Rainbow" played. One of my favorite memories, with each of my children, is lightly rubbing their backs as they drift off to sleep, always to the tune of this classic song. My heart overflows when I'm able to love my people in ways I know connect with their hearts.

Those moments don't happen by accident,

though. The blinds were pulled just right, the bed pulled down just so, and the song made to play at just the right time—so that my little buddy could feel this moment of quiet, pure love from his mama. I'm not sure anything makes me feel more whole or proud than seeing his squished little smile as I run my fingers up and down his back and his eyes get heavier and heavier.

The first time I took an Enneagram test, I wasn't even sure what it was. I assumed it was a personality test that would help me better understand my personality traits. What I didn't realize was that understanding my Enneagram Type would help me feel more secure about my quirky qualities, my secret fears, and the true longings of my heart.

When I learned that I'm an Enneagram Type 2, I felt so understood. Finally, my lifelong desire to serve and love, above all else, made sense. Everyone knew that about me, so the results of the test didn't come as a surprise. But not everyone knew how much I struggled with perfectionism, with a thirst for affection and recognition, and with my own need to control certain situations. The Enneagram helped validate some of those feelings and has given me a bit of freedom from them now that I know how much my weaknesses actually correlate to my strengths.

My husband of eleven years took an Enneagram test shortly after I did. We've always laughed that we are polar opposites, so I expected him to be on the opposite side of the spectrum. I love big salads and seafood. He loves mashed potatoes and steak. I'm a planner. He's spontaneous. We were shocked to learn that I am Type 2 with a 3 wing, he is Type 3 with a 4 wing. We actually share many similarities! Continuing to learn about how our Types interact, at their best and at their worst, has been fascinating and enlightening.

I also have a team of eight women who help me run our brand of planners and organizational tools, Simplified®. Each of my team members took the test, and we learned how we all fit together. We're all over the spectrum! Knowing how to balance our strengths and weaknesses has made me a better leader. And it has helped us serve our customers even better by having the right people in the right roles.

If you are also Type 2, or are here to learn more about Type 2s, welcome! I'm honored to introduce you to this book. In typical Type 2 fashion, I'd love to invite you to settle in, take off your shoes, grab a cup of tea, and stay a while with us. We're great hosts, and we're glad you're here.

Emily Ley, Founder of Simplified®,
Bestselling Author of *Grace, Not Perfection*

Introduction

I'm so glad you're here! As an Enneagram teacher and coach, I have seen so many lives changed by the Enneagram. This is a perfect place for you to start your own journey of growth. I'll explain how this interactive book works, but first I'd like to share a little of my story.

Before I learned about the Enneagram, I often unknowingly committed *assumicide*, which is my word for damaging a relationship by assuming I know someone's thoughts, feelings, and motivations. I incorrectly surmise why someone is behaving a particular way and respond (sometimes with disastrous results) without asking clarifying questions to confirm my assumptions or to find out what actually is going on. I've made many wrong and hurtful assumptions about people I dearly love, as well as destructive presumptions about myself.

When my husband, Jeff, and I were in the early years of our marriage, it was a difficult season in our relationship. For the life of me, I couldn't figure out Jeff, or myself. I had been a Christian since I was young and desired to live like Christ, but I kept running into the same stumbling blocks over and over again. I was constantly frustrated, and I longed to understand my heart's motives—*Why do I do what I do?* I figured understanding that might help jolt me out of my rut, but I didn't know where to start.

Then I learned about the insightful tool of the Enneagram, and it was exactly what I needed.

This personality typology (*ennea* for nine; *gram* for diagram) goes beyond what we do (our behaviors) and gets at *why* we do what we do (our heart's motives). And though there are just nine basic personality Types, each Type has multiple layers, allowing for numerous variations of any given personality Type.

The purpose of the Enneagram is to awaken self-awareness and provide hope for growth. Once we learn why each Type thinks, feels, and acts in specific ways, we can look at ourselves with new understanding. Then we can depend on God in new ways to reshape us. The Enneagram makes us aware of when our heart's motives are good and we are on the best path for our personality Type, and when our heart is struggling and veering off course. The Enneagram is an insightful tool, but God's truth is what sets us free and brings transformation.

When I first learned about the Enneagram, I resonated with the Type 9—and had a good laugh when I discovered that 9s know themselves the least! But I finally had wisdom that cleared away the fog and illuminated my inner world. I kept thinking, *Oh, that's why I do that!* Everything started making sense, which brought my restless heart relief.

The Enneagram also helped me see when my heart was aligned with God's truth, misaligned to some degree, or out of alignment entirely with the person God created me to be. It would highlight where I was misunderstanding myself or those I love, and then I could use that awareness to seek transformation. Using the Enneagram from this perspective was a significant turning point for me in all my relationships, especially my marriage. My new perspective allowed me to have more compassion, kindness, forgiveness, mercy, and grace toward others and myself.

Exploring my heart has been some of the hardest—and most rewarding—work I've ever done. The process of looking at our hearts exposes who we are at the core, which highlights our need for redemption and care from God, who is always supplying us with what we need. We simply need to come to Him and depend on Him to change us from the inside out. He will give us a new internal peace, joy, and security that will help us to flourish in new and life-giving ways. The Enneagram can function as an internal GPS, helping you understand why you and others think, feel, and behave in particular ways.

This internal GPS assists you in knowing your current location (your Main Enneagram Type) and your Type's healthiest destination (how your Type can live in alignment with the gospel).

The Enneagram also acts like a rumble strip on the highway—that boundary that makes an irritating sound when your car touches it, warning you when you're about to go off course. It keeps you from swerving into dangerous situations.

While everyone has character traits of all nine Types to varying degrees, we call only one our Main Type. In this book you will unlock some of the mysteries behind *why* you do what you do and discern ways you can grow into your best self.

If you're not sure of your Type number, that's okay! Going through the exercises will help you figure out what your Type number is. Sometimes it's helpful to find out what we're *not* as much as what we are. It's all about self-discovery and self-awareness.

If you find you resonate more with another number, that insight is valuable.

• • •

In the twenty-one entries that follow, we'll begin with a summary of your Type. Then we'll discuss topics that are general to the Enneagram and specific to your Type. Each reading will end with reflection questions—prompts to help you write out your thoughts, feelings, and gut reactions to what you have read. Putting pen to paper will help you focus and process what is going on inside you.

Before you begin, I want you to commit to observing your inner world from a nonjudgmental stance. Since God has fully forgiven us, we can observe ourselves without condemnation, guilt, or shame. Instead, we can rest in the fact that we are unconditionally loved, forgiven, and accepted based on what Christ did for us. Follow the prompts and write about your own story. Allow God to transform you from the inside out by helping you see yourself through the lens of the beautiful and amazing Type He designed you to be.

It's my privilege to walk with you as you discover who you are by examining your heart. I'm excited to be on this journey with you!

You are encouraging, supportive, and able to see the good in me. You are nurturing, generous, giving, and loving. You are also thoughtful, warm-hearted, forgiving, and a deep well of compassion that blesses me.

OVERVIEW OF THE NINE ENNEAGRAM TYPES

The Enneagram (*ennea* = nine, *gram* = diagram) is a map for personal growth that identifies the nine basic ways of relating to and perceiving the world. It accurately describes *why* you think, feel, and behave in particular ways based upon your Core Motivations. Understanding the Enneagram will give you more self-awareness, forgiveness, and compassion for yourself and others.

To find your main Type, take our FREE assessment at test.YourEnneagramCoach.com, and find the Type on the next page that has your Core Motivations— what activates and drives your thoughts, feelings, and behaviors.

Core Motivations of Each Type

Core Desires: what you're always striving for, believing it will completely fulfill you

Core Fears: what you're always avoiding and trying to prevent from happening

Core Weakness: the issue you're always wrestling with, which will remain a struggle until you're in heaven and is a reminder you need God's help on a daily basis

Core Longing: the message your heart is always longing to hear

Type 1: MORAL PERFECTIONIST

Core Desire: Having integrity; being good, balanced, accurate, virtuous, and right.

Core Fear: Being wrong, bad, evil, inappropriate, unredeemable, or corruptible.

Core Weakness: *Resentment*: Repressing anger that leads to continual frustration and dissatisfaction with yourself, others, and the world for not being perfect.

Core Longing: You are good.

Type 2: SUPPORTIVE ADVISOR

☀ **Core Desire:** Being appreciated, loved, and wanted.

⚡ **Core Fear:** Being rejected and unwanted; being thought worthless, needy, inconsequential, dispensable, or unworthy of love.

☄ **Core Weakness:** *Pride*: Denying your own needs and emotions while using your strong intuition to discover and focus on the emotions and needs of others; confidently inserting your helpful support in hopes that others will say how grateful they are for your thoughtful care.

🔥 **Core Longing:** You are wanted and loved.

Type 3: SUCCESSFUL ACHIEVER

☀ **Core Desire:** Having high status and respect; being admired, successful, and valuable.

⚡ **Core Fear:** Being exposed as or thought incompetent, inefficient, or worthless; failing to be or appear successful.

☄ **Core Weakness:** *Deceit*: Deceiving yourself into believing that you are only the image you present to others; embellishing the truth by putting on a polished persona for everyone (including yourself) to see and admire.

🔥 **Core Longing:** You are loved for simply being you.

Type 4: ROMANTIC INDIVIDUALIST

☀ **Core Desire:** Being unique, special, and authentic.

❗ **Core Fear:** Being inadequate, emotionally cut off, plain, mundane, defective, flawed, or insignificant.

🗯 **Core Weakness:** *Envy:* Feeling that you're tragically flawed, that something foundational is missing inside you, and that others possess qualities you lack.

🔥 **Core Longing:** You are seen and loved for exactly who you are—special and unique.

Type 5: INVESTIGATIVE THINKER

☀ **Core Desire:** Being capable and competent.

❗ **Core Fear:** Being annihilated, invaded, or not existing; being thought incapable or ignorant; having obligations placed upon you, or your energy being completely depleted.

🗯 **Core Weakness:** *Avarice:* Feeling that you lack inner resources and that too much interaction with others will lead to catastrophic depletion; withholding yourself from contact with the world; holding on to your resources and minimizing your needs.

🔥 **Core Longing:** Your needs are not a problem.

Type 6: LOYAL GUARDIAN

Core Desire: Having security, guidance, and support.

Core Fear: Fearing fear itself; being without support, security, or guidance; being blamed, targeted, alone, or physically abandoned.

Core Weakness: *Anxiety*: Scanning the horizon of life and trying to predict and prevent negative outcomes (especially worst-case scenarios); remaining in a constant state of apprehension and worry.

Core Longing: You are safe and secure.

Type 7: ENTERTAINING OPTIMIST

Core Desire: Being happy, fully satisfied, and content.

Core Fear: Being deprived, trapped in emotional pain, limited, or bored; missing out on something fun.

Core Weakness: *Gluttony*: Feeling a great emptiness inside and having an insatiable desire to "fill yourself up" with experiences and stimulation in hopes of feeling completely satisfied and content.

Core Longing: You will be taken care of.

Type 8: PROTECTIVE CHALLENGER

☀ **Core Desire:** Protecting yourself and those in your inner circle.

⚠ **Core Fear:** Being weak, powerless, harmed, controlled, vulnerable, manipulated, and left at the mercy of injustice.

💢 **Core Weakness:** *Lust/Excess*: Constantly desiring intensity, control, and power; willfully pushing yourself on others in order to get what you desire.

🔥 **Core Longing:** You will not be betrayed.

Type 9: PEACEFUL MEDIATOR

☀ **Core Desire:** Having inner stability and peace of mind.

⚠ **Core Fear:** Being in conflict, tension, or discord; feeling shut out and overlooked; losing connection and relationship with others.

💢 **Core Weakness:** *Sloth*: Remaining in an unrealistic and idealistic world in order to keep the peace, remain easygoing, and not be disturbed by your anger; falling asleep to your passions, abilities, desires, needs, and worth by merging with others to keep peace and harmony.

🔥 **Core Longing:** Your presence matters.

TYPE 2
KEY MOTIVATIONS

Type 2s want to be loved, wanted, and appreciated. They also want to express what they feel for others by helping, serving, and supporting the needs of others in hopes of hearing the appreciation, affection, and affirmation from those they serve.

Overview of Type 2

The Supportive Advisor

Thoughtful | Generous | Demonstrative
People-Pleasing | Possessive

You walk through life prioritizing relationships, making sure the people around you always feel well-cared for and loved. You take a genuine interest in others and come alongside anyone in need, offering acts of service, helpful advice, and nurture.

However, because you are so empathetic and sensitive, the depth of need and suffering in our world is especially burdensome to you. You feel that it is your job to alleviate the pain of hurting people around you, which is an unending responsibility.

You seek satisfaction by trying to help others because deep down you struggle to believe that others love you apart from the support you offer. In your attempt to fulfill this longing to be loved by looking to others instead of God, you can become people-pleasing and possessive. You may insert yourself into the lives of others, violating boundaries.

This overwhelming burden to care for everyone is damaging when you begin to attend to others' needs without adequately dealing with your own. In your pride, you may believe you know what's best and can take care of everyone while denying the care you need.

Relationally, you may struggle when others feel crowded by your efforts to help. You may feel hurt and insecure when you aren't needed and double down on your efforts to win people over.

However, when your heart aligns with God's truth and you learn to take your longings to Him, you experience transformation by trusting that you are wanted and loved apart from what you can do for others. As you tend to your own needs, your heart is strengthened and able to offer selfless generosity, encouragement, and redemptive kindness to the world.

Faith and the Enneagram

Is your heart a mystery to you? Do you need help using the knowledge the Enneagram offers to improve your life? If that's where you are, I'm happy to tell you that there is help and there is hope.

The Bible teaches that God cares about our heart's motives. He "sees not as man sees: man looks on the outward appearance, but the LORD looks on the heart" (1 Samuel 16:7). So we shouldn't look only at our external behaviors; we also need to examine our inner world. For most of us, it's no surprise that the heart of our problem is the problem of our heart!

Before we begin discussing the Enneagram in depth, I'd like to share my beliefs with you for two reasons: First, it's a critical part of how I'll guide you through the Enneagram principles. Second, my faith is what sustains and encourages me, and I believe the same will be true for you.

I believe the Bible is God's truth and the ultimate authority for our lives. Through it, we learn about God's character, love, and wisdom. It brings us close to Him and guides us in the best way to live. My relationship with God brought me healing and purpose before I ever heard of the Enneagram.

Jesus has not been optional for my personal growth; He has been absolutely and utterly vital. He has always come alongside me with love, compassion, and mercy.

I've always wanted my faith to be the most important part of my life, but I spent years frustrated, running into the same issues in my heart over and over again. The Enneagram helped me understand my heart's motives.

As you think about your Type, I'll help you look

at your heart, your life, and your relationships through the lens of the Enneagram. I'll also teach you ways to understand yourself and others and to develop patience and empathy for your differences.

With God working in you and helpful insights from the Enneagram to change awareness and actions, you'll grow into the person you'd like to be more than you've ever dared to dream possible.

When you place your faith in Jesus Christ as your Savior, three life-changing questions are answered, bringing you ultimate grace and freedom:

Am I fully accepted by God (even with all the mess and sin in my life)?

Yes! You are declared righteous. Christ not only purchased forgiveness for your sin but also gave you His perfect righteousness.

Am I loved by God?

Yes! God cherishes you and wants you to be close to Him. He adopted you, making you His beloved child.

Is it really possible for me to change?

Yes! You are being made new. This both *happened* to you and *is happening* to you. This means that you are changed because of what Christ has done, and you are continuing to change as you grow in Christ (it's a bit of a paradox). You can live in an ongoing process of growth by working with the Holy Spirit to become more like Christ, who loves you and gave Himself up for you.

These three life-changing events are what we mean by God's truth, the good news of Christ's finished work on our behalf—"the gospel."

Receiving God's truth and learning about the Enneagram will give you a deeper and richer understanding of *who you are* and *Whose you are*.

When we know *who we are*, we understand our heart's motives and needs and can see God reaching out to meet our needs and giving us grace for our sins through Christ.

And when we know *Whose we are*, we understand that because of Christ's sacrifice on our behalf, we're God's cherished children. He comforts, sustains, and delights in us. Because of God's character, His love never changes; it doesn't depend on us "getting better" or "doing better" since it hinges solely on what Christ has already done for us. He loves us and desires for us to be in a relationship with Him. We become more like Him by surrendering to Him and depending on the Holy Spirit to transform us.

Which leads us back to looking at who we are. Bringing our faith and the Enneagram together helps us hear God's truths in our mother tongue (kind of like our personality Type's unique language), which enables us to understand God's truth more deeply and will lead to transformation.

Going Deeper

What things have you longed to change about yourself?

_____

_____

_____

_____

_____

_____

_____

_____

How have you attempted to rescue yourself in the past or bring about change on your own? How successful were you?

_____

_____

_____

_____

What difference does knowing you belong to God make in your life?

Being Aware

We can't do anything to make God love us more or love us less since our relationship status has been taken care of solely through Christ's finished work on our behalf. And yet that doesn't mean we're not responsible for participating in our growth. That growth path will look different for different personality Types. We can use the Enneagram to help us find our unique path for transformation as we continue learning and growing. And that's what's super fun about the Enneagram! This insightful tool helps us discover *who we are* and *Whose we are.*

We are not alone on this journey of growth.

God is with us, sustaining us and providing for us. Although we're all uniquely made and no one is alike (it boggles the mind to think about it!), there are commonalities in how we think, feel, and act. The Enneagram shows us nine basic personality Types, each with its own specific patterns of thinking and ways of being: nine *valid* perspectives of the world. Getting to know each of these personality Types increases understanding, compassion, mercy, grace, and forgiveness toward ourselves and others.

Our creative God made us so diverse, yet we all reflect the essence of His character: wise, caring, radiant, creative, knowledgeable, insightful, joyful, protective, and peaceful. As we learn about ourselves and others from the Enneagram, we also learn more about God. Our strengths reflect His attributes.

So how do we begin to find our unique path for growth? By learning about the Enneagram, and by becoming aware of how our heart is doing, which isn't always easy for us. It takes a great deal of time and intentional focus. We start by observing our inner world from a *nonjudgmental* stance. (I don't know how to emphasize this enough!)

Then we can begin to recognize patterns, pause while we are in the present circumstance, and ask ourselves good, clarifying questions about *why* we are thinking, feeling, or behaving in particular ways. We can begin to identify those frustrating patterns we repeat over and over again (the ones we haven't been able to figure out how to stop) and start to think about why we keep doing them.

As I've said before, the Enneagram can act like a rumble strip on a highway, warning you when you're heading off your best path. It lets you know that if you continue in the same direction, drowsy or distracted, you might hurt yourself and others. Alerts about impending danger will allow you to course correct, avoid heartache, and experience greater freedom. You will create new patterns of behavior, including a new way of turning to God, when you start to notice the rumble strips in your life.

When you're sensing a rumble strip warning, focus on the acronym AWARE:

- *Awaken*: Notice how you are reacting in your behavior, feelings, thoughts, and body sensations.
- *Welcome*: Be open to what you might learn and observe without condemnation and shame.
- *Ask*: Ask God to help clarify what is happening internally.
- *Receive*: Receive any insight and affirm your true identity as God's beloved child.
- *Enjoy*: Enjoy your new freedom from old self-defeating patterns of living.

Going Deeper

As you look back on your life, when would you have liked a rumble strip to warn you of danger?

In general, what causes you to veer off course and land in a common pitfall (for example, when you're worried)?

SHARING WITH OTHERS HOW BEST TO LOVE ME

Tell me specifically what you appreciate about me.

Take a real interest in my problems, even though I will try to focus the attention back to you.

Please let me know that I am special and important to you. Tell me what you love about me.

If you need to point out something negative, please be gentle and tell me a few affirming things as well. I can be very sensitive to criticism.

Enjoy sharing fun times with me.

Core Motivations

We'll begin discussing the fundamentals of the Enneagram by looking at our motivations.

Your Core Motivations are the driving force behind your thoughts, feelings, and actions. The internal motivations specific to your Type help explain why you do what you do. (This is why it's impossible to discern someone else's Type. We don't know what motivates them to think, feel, and behave in particular ways. It's their Core Motivations, not their actions, that determine their Type.)

These Core Motivations consist of:

- *Core Fear*: what you're always avoiding and trying to prevent from happening
- *Core Desire*: what you're always striving for, believing it will completely fulfill you
- *Core Weakness*: the issue you're always wrestling with, which will remain a struggle until you're in heaven and is a reminder you need God's help on a daily basis
- *Core Longing*: the message your heart longs to hear

The Enneagram, like a nonjudgmental friend, names and addresses these dynamics of your heart. When you use the Enneagram from a faith-centered approach, you can see how Christ's finished work on your behalf has already satisfied your Core Longing and resolved your Core Fear, Core Desire, and Core Weakness. It's a process to learn how to live in to that reality.

When we stray from the truth that we are God's beloved children, it's harder to look inside. After all,

Scripture tells us that "the heart is deceitful . . . and desperately sick" (Jeremiah 17:9). When we forget God's unconditional love for us, we respond to our weaknesses and vulnerabilities with shame or contempt, leaving us feeling worse.

When we only focus on obeying externally, we attempt to look good on the outside but never deal with the source of all our struggles on the inside.

However, when we allow ourselves to rest in the truth that Christ took care of everything for us, we can look at our inner world without fear or condemnation. Real transformation begins when we own our shortcomings.

Here are the Core Motivations of a Type 2:

- *Core Fear*: being rejected and unwanted; being thought worthless, needy, inconsequential, dispensable, or unworthy of love
- *Core Desire*: being appreciated, loved, and wanted
- *Core Weakness*: pride; denying your own

needs and emotions while using your strong intuition to discover and focus on the emotions and needs of others; confidently inserting your helpful support in hopes that others will say how grateful they are for your thoughtful care

- *Core Longing*: "You are wanted and loved."

The Enneagram exposes the condition of our hearts, and it will tear down any facade we try to hide behind. Since we are God's saved children, we don't have to be afraid of judgment. We can be vulnerable because we know God has taken care of us perfectly through Christ—He has forgiven us and set us free from fear, condemnation, and shame. His presence is a safe place where we can be completely honest about where we are. With this freedom, allow the Enneagram to be a flashlight to your heart's condition. Let it reveal how you are doing at any given moment so you can remain on the best path for your personality Type.

Going Deeper

How challenging is it for you to look at the condition of your heart?

_____

_____

_____

_____

_____

_____

What response do you typically have when you recognize your struggles?

_____

_____

_____

_____

_____

_____

How would you like to respond when the struggles inside you are exposed?

Core Fear

Understanding your Core Fear is the first step in identifying your motivations. Your personality believes it's vital to your well-being that you constantly spend time and energy avoiding this thing you fear. It is the lens through which you see the world, the "reality" you believe. You assume others do, or should, see the world through this lens, and you may become confused and dismayed when they don't.

Your Core Fear as a Type 2 is being rejected and unwanted; being thought worthless, needy, inconsequential, dispensable, or unworthy of love.

You don't want to feel left out or without

connection to others. You are convinced that if you acknowledge and take care of your own needs (emotional, relational, or physical), it will jeopardize your relationships because others might view you as selfish and reject you.

Even though you fear being unwanted or unworthy of love, here's what is actually true: God desires to be with you. He created the universe. He is all-powerful, all-knowing, all-providing, and all-sustaining. He is good, and He wants you, personally, to be in close relationship with Him. When you were far from Him, He pursued you, demonstrating His great love for you. He has called you valuable, treasured, and cherished.

When your Core Fears get activated, use them as a rumble strip to alert you. Then pause, become AWARE, and reorient yourself with what is true so your heart can rest in His care for you.

MY CORE FEARS

TYPE 2
THE SUPPORTIVE
ADVISOR

Being rejected and unwanted; being thought worthless, needy, inconsequential, dispensable, or unworthy of love

Going Deeper

What comes to mind when you think about your Core Fear?

_____

_____

_____

_____

_____

_____

_____

_____

_____

Do any particular words in the Type 2 Core Fear description ring true for you?

_____

_____

_____

_____

_____

What strategies have you used in the past to
protect yourself from your fears?

Core Desire

Understanding your Core Desire is the next step in identifying your motivations. Your Core Desire is what you're always striving for, believing it will ultimately fulfill you.

While your personality Type is running away from your Core Fear, it's also running toward your Core Desire. You believe that once you have this Core Desire met, all of life will be okay and you will feel fully satisfied and content. This longing to experience your Core Desire constantly propels you to focus your efforts on pursuing and obtaining it.

As a Type 2, you desire to be appreciated, loved, and wanted.

God knows your Core Desire, and He freely gives it to you. You are valuable to Him beyond compare! He pursues you with His unending love and sees you as His cherished child. He truly delights in you.

God desires to be close to you and has provided a way through Christ for that to be possible. You can rest in the fact that He extends acceptance and love to you every day, no matter what.

Not everyone has the same Core Desire as you. Take time to recognize that others are just as passionate in obtaining their Core Desire as you are in gaining yours. This awareness will help you navigate relationship dynamics, enabling you to offer more empathy, compassion, and grace. Use the Enneagram to know yourself better so you can better communicate with others about what is happening inside your heart. Then be curious about others, and ask them to reveal to you their desires so you can get to know them on a deeper level.

**MY CORE
DESIRES**

TYPE 2
THE SUPPORTIVE
ADVISOR

Being appreciated, loved, and wanted

Going Deeper

As you look back over your life, what aspects of the Type 2 Core Desire have you been chasing?

_____

_____

_____

_____

Describe ways you have attempted to pursue these specific desires.

_____

_____

_____

_____

What would it feel like to trust in the fact that God has already met your Core Desire?

_____

_____

_____

_____

Core Weakness

Deep inside, you struggle with a Core Weakness, which is your Achilles' heel. This one issue repeatedly causes you to stumble in life. At times you might find some relief. But as hard as you try to improve on your own, your struggle in this area continually resurfaces.

God's encouraging words to you are that when you are weak, He is strong. This brings hope that you are not destined to be utterly stuck in your weakness. As you grow closer to God and depend on Him, He will lessen the constraint your Core Weakness has over you and help you move out of your rut.

As a Type 2, your Core Weakness is *pride*. You deny your own needs and emotions while using your strong intuition to discover and focus on the needs and emotions of others. You confidently insert your support into others' lives, hoping they will acknowledge how grateful they are for you.

You don't believe it's possible others will unconditionally love you just for being you, so you are compelled to earn their approval by feeling their emotions and meeting their needs through selfless care. You avoid acknowledging your own needs since you believe others will think you're selfish and reject you for doing so.

However, when you grasp the depth of God's love and desire for you, you will experience the freedom to take care of yourself. Out of the overflow of love you receive from Him, you can care for others, and then be replenished by His love. You will no longer need to prove your worth to others since you will be basking in the full, unconditional love of God.

Earning praise from other people cannot bring

real satisfaction. In true humility, acknowledge that you were created with needs intended to be fulfilled by God, and turn to Him to receive what your heart longs for.

When you see your Core Weakness surfacing, think of it as a rumble strip, alerting you that you can easily veer off course into your common pitfalls of denying your own needs and solely focusing on the needs of others, even if it is not asked for or wanted. Use this awareness to "recalculate" your inner world so you can get back to your healthiest path.

Going Deeper

What comes to mind as you think about your Core Weakness?

In what ways have you wrestled with pride throughout your life?

_____

_____

_____

_____

_____

_____

_____

What specific things are you facing now that your Core Weakness impacts?

_____

_____

_____

_____

_____

_____

_____

MY CORE WEAKNESS

TYPE 2
THE SUPPORTIVE ADVISOR

Pride — denying your own needs and emotions while using your strong intuition to discover and focus on the emotions and needs of others; confidently inserting your helpful support in hopes that others will say how grateful they are for your thoughtful care

Core Longing

Your Core Longing is the message your heart is always yearning to receive, what you've craved since you were a child. Throughout life, you've been striving to hear this message from your family members, friends, teachers, coaches, and bosses. No matter how much you've tried to get others to communicate this message to you, you've never felt it was delivered to the degree your heart needed it.

As a Type 2, your Core Longing is to hear, "You are wanted and loved."

You have believed that if you could be caring, nurturing, and selfless enough, then others would communicate this message to you, whether in verbal or nonverbal ways. However, even those who have tried their best to do this for you are unable to satisfy this longing that runs so deep inside you.

Why? Because people *cannot* give you all you need. Only God can. When you're trying to receive this message apart from God, you will always thirst for more. But when you listen to Him and see that He's drawing you to Himself, then you will find fulfillment and freedom.

How does God meet your Core Longing?

1. **He wants to be with you.**

    Jesus left heaven and came to earth because He wanted to save you and have you with Him. You are so valuable to Him that He laid down His own life for you. You are wanted!

2. **He loves you.**

    Jesus demonstrated the ultimate act of care, support, and love by sacrificing Himself for you. When you were far from Him, He sought you out to offer you healing and closeness with Him—because He loves you!

When you feel rejected and unloved, use the Enneagram as the rumble strip to alert you of what is true: that you are wanted and loved by God. Allow it to point out how you are believing false messages so you can live a more fulfilling and joyful life.

Going Deeper

How have you seen your Core Longing at work in your life?

What did that look like when you were a child?

_____

_____

_____

_____

_____

_____

_____

_____

_____

_____

_____

How does it appear in your life as an adult?

_____

_____

_____

_____

_____

_____

Describe how you feel and what you think when you read that God answers your longing.

MY CORE LONGING   **TYPE 2**
THE SUPPORTIVE
ADVISOR

The message my heart always longs to hear.

"You are wanted and loved
for just being you."

Directional Signals of the Enneagram

Just as a GPS gives directional signals such as "Approaching right turn" or "Proceed to the high-lighted route," the Enneagram guides us in which way to go. But we still need to pay attention to where we're heading and reroute our course when necessary.

The Enneagram provides directions in a couple of ways: (1) by pointing out how aligned with God's truth we are, and (2) by showing us what other Types we are connected to and how we might take on those Types' characteristics in different life situations. We do not *become* the Types we are

HOW TO USE THE ENNEAGRAM
YOUR INTERNAL GPS

It reveals *why* you think, feel, and behave in particular ways, so you can steer your internal life in the best direction for your personality Type.

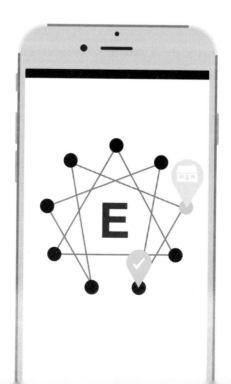

connected to; we remain our Main Type (with its Core Fear, Desire, Weakness, and Longing) as we access the other Types' attributes.

The directional signals of the Enneagram make us aware of which way our heart is heading and where we might end up. Whether it's a good or bad direction depends on various factors—it can change day by day as we take on positive or negative qualities of other Types.

When we are headed in the wrong direction, the steps to turning around and getting back on track are simply owning our mistakes, turning from them, asking for forgiveness from God and others, and asking God to restore us to the best path.

The directional signals we'll discuss in the following entries are: the Levels of Alignment with God's Truth, the Wings, the Triads, and the Enneagram Paths. Hang in there! I'll guide you through these signals, which will help you discover who you are and Whose you are, and show you the healthiest path for your personality Type.

Type 2

HOW I TYPICALLY COMMUNICATE

When I am doing well, I am a warm presence. I listen to others carefully, ask good questions, and give helpful guidance. I am a compassionate and empathetic listener.

When I am not doing well, I can be either passive-aggressive or very direct and give unsolicited advice. When I am "helping" too much, I can get angry and complain.

Levels of Alignment
with God's Truth

The first set of directional signals we'll discuss are the Levels of Alignment with God's truth. The inspiration for these levels comes from the apostle Paul, who wrote in Galatians 2:14 that some of the early Christian leaders' conduct was not in step (aligned) with God's truth. To grow in our particular personality Type, we must be in step with God's truth and design for us.

We all move fluidly through the Levels of Alignment from day to day. The level at which we find ourselves at any given moment depends on our heart's condition and how we're navigating through life.

Healthy	Aligned with God's Truth (Living as His Beloved)
Average (Autopilot)	Misaligned with God's Truth (Living in Our Own Strength)
Unhealthy	Out of Alignment with God's Truth (Living as an Orphan)

When we are resting, believing, and trusting in who we are in Christ, we are living as His beloved (healthy and aligned with God's truth). We are no longer using our personality strategies to meet our needs and desires. Instead, we are coming to our God, who we know loves us and will provide for us.

When our heart and mind begin to wander from that truth, we start to believe that we must take some control and live in our own strength, even though He is good and sovereign (average/auto-pilot level).

Then there are times when we completely forget that we are His beloved children. In this state of mind, we think we're all alone, that we're orphans who have to handle all of life on our own (unhealthy level).

But no matter where we are on the Levels of Alignment, we are always His cherished children. Christ's life, death, and resurrection accomplished everything required for us to be His. Therefore, no matter what state our heart is in, we can *rejoice* in His work in our lives, *repent* if we need to, and fully *rest* in who we are in Him.

As you can imagine, a group of people with the same personality Type (same Core Fear, Desire, Weakness, and Longing) can look vastly different from each other due to varying alignments with God's truth.

In the readings that follow, we will consider how you as a Type 2 function at the three Levels of Alignment.

Going Deeper

At what Level of Alignment do you think your heart is at the moment?

In what season of life have you thrived the most, not feeling limited by your fears and weaknesses?

What do you think contributed to that growth?

When You Are Aligned

When the condition of your heart is healthy, you align with God's truth that you are fully taken care of by Christ.

As a Type 2 at this level, you are deeply unselfish, humble, and kind, giving unconditional love to yourself and others. You feel it is a privilege to be in the lives of others *without* needing them to come through for you. You trust that you are loved and wanted by God, which frees you to acknowledge your own needs and maintain appropriate boundaries by saying no to helping others when it is not your responsibility.

You are empathetic and compassionate and feel

strongly for others. In a healthy emotional condition, you serve them not to gain approval and love for yourself, but out of genuine care for them, displaying the love and nurture of God. You are thoughtful, warmhearted, forgiving, and sincere.

While service is important to you, you also are aware of your own needs and can tend to them. Taking care of yourself allows you to serve others better.

Going Deeper

When are you at your best and most trusting of God?

_____

_____

_____

_____

_____

_____

What differences do you notice in your thinking and in your life when you're in that state?

What helps you stay in alignment with God's plan for your personality Type?

Write about a time when you've exhibited equal focus on others and your needs and giving freely without needing anything in return.

When You Are Misaligned

Even though we know God is good and in control, there are times when our hearts and minds wander away from the truth that God loves us and has fully provided for us in the finished work of Christ on our behalf. In this average or autopilot level of health, we start to believe that we must take some control and live in our own strength.

As a Type 2 at this level, you invest time and energy into anything that will bring you love and appreciation. Feeling the need to be close to others, you start people-pleasing, becoming overly friendly, and emotionally demonstrative. You may give seductive attention (perhaps approval or

MY HIDDEN STRUGGLE
TYPE 2

An insatiable yearning for the
approval, appreciation, and
acceptance of others

The effort to be a source of emotional
stability in every relationship, and
weariness from giving constant
help and support

The feeling that others don't
appreciate my efforts, leading to
rejection, disappointment,
and resentment

flattery) to win people over. You believe you are full of good intentions in everything you do for others.

You can become overly intimate and intrusive in your relationships, needing to be needed. So you hover, meddle, and control in the name of love. Longing to have others depend on you, you give to get appreciation. You will wear yourself out by sacrificing yourself for everyone, hoping to receive their affirmation.

As you double down on your efforts to earn love, you may feel you're indispensable and act as a martyr for others. You also can be overbearing, patronizing, and presumptuous when you don't get the gratitude you feel you deserve.

Going Deeper

What aspects of your behavior and life indicate that you are becoming misaligned?

In what ways do you attempt to live in your own strength, not in your identity as a person God loves?

What can you do when you begin to catch yourself in misalignment?

When You Are Out of Alignment Entirely

When we completely forget that our status never changes and we are still His beloved based on what Christ did for us, we think and believe we're all alone, like an orphan.

As a Type 2 at this level, you believe your whole worth revolves around others' opinions of you. To feel you are connected with others, you search for those who need help and intervene, even if your help is not invited or wanted. You become like a martyr, hoping others will see you as the ultimate giver.

The problem is that there is nothing you will

not do to hear words of affirmation from others. This pursuit exhausts you and can lead to physical illness. If your efforts are not acknowledged, you will feel hurt and rejected, which will spark resentment in your heart. You may punish others by being passive-aggressive or actively aggressive, controlling, and demanding.

This cycle will continue until you realize that God is a loving and caring Father to you. When you begin to believe this truth and depend on Him completely, you will move up the levels of health.

Going Deeper

In what seasons of life have you been most out of alignment with God's truth?

What does this level look like for you (specific behaviors, beliefs, etc.)?

Who in your life can best support and encourage you when you're struggling and guide you back to health?

The Wings

The next set of directional signals we'll discuss are the Wings, which are the two numbers *directly* next to your Main Type's number on the Enneagram diagram. As I've said, we access the characteristics of the Type on either side of us while remaining our Main Type. So everyone's Enneagram personality is a combination of one Main Type and the two Types adjacent to it.

As a Type 2, your Wings are 1 and 3. You'll often see it written this way: 2w1 or 2w3.

Everyone uses their Wings to varying degrees and differently in different circumstances, but it's common for a person to rely more on one Wing than another.

You can think of the Wings like salt and pepper. Each Wing adds a unique "flavor" to your personality, bringing complexity to your Main Type. Just as a delicious filet mignon doesn't *become* the salt or pepper we season it with, we don't become our Wings. Our Wings influence our Main Type in varying ways, both positively and negatively depending on where we are on the Levels of Alignment. We know that too much salt or pepper can make that filet inedible, but the right balance can enhance our enjoyment of it significantly.

When we align with God's truth, we can access the healthy aspects of our Wings. When we are misaligned or out of alignment with God's truth, we will often draw from the average or unhealthy aspects of our Wings. And like under seasoning or over seasoning our perfectly cooked steaks, it can make a huge difference.

Learning how to use our Wings correctly can dramatically alter our life experiences. Applying "seasoning"—utilizing the healthy attributes of our Wings—can help us change course. As we return to believing and trusting in God, we can express ourselves more fully and be seen for who we really are.

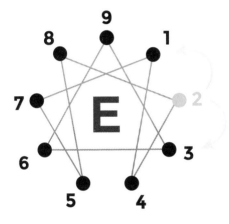

Type 2 with Wing 1 (2w1), The Servant: Type 1 brings more emotional self-control, objectivity, and seriousness to Type 2.

If you're a Servant, you have a strong sense of responsibility and the need to do what is right for others (which means you can be mistyped as a Type 6). You focus on improving the lives of others by serving them and are driven by helping them see what is right and good. You can be an excellent teacher by offering a combination of principles, values, encouragement, and warmth.

When you are struggling, you may insist others follow your moral advice. Others can feel controlled by the intensity of your virtues. You also can struggle with self-condemnation and guilt, more so than the Host/Hostess does.

Type 2 with Wing 3 (2w3), The Host/Hostess: These two types blend easily. They are both personable, charming, and adaptable, and desire to be liked and valued.

If you're a Host/Hostess, you are sociable and self-assured. You exude a charming friendliness and bless others with your talents (such as cooking, entertaining, or bringing social connection to a group) more than through serving quietly. You are a likable and outgoing person who enjoys the spotlight and attention.

Wanting to be perceived as desirable, you focus on your physical attractiveness (not on moral

Type 2 WINGS

Type 2 with 1 Wing (2w1)
"Servant"
They tend to be more idealistic, reasonable, objective, self-critical, quietly serving, and judgmental.

Type 2 with 3 Wing (2w3)
"Host/Hostess"
They tend to be more self-assured, charming, a flatterer, ambitious, outgoing, and competitive.

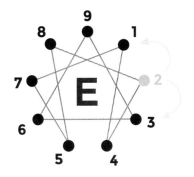

perfection, like the Servant) and are overly affirming to others. It is also important for you to have impressive and popular friends who boost your image.

Going Deeper

Which Wing do you use more?

_____

_____

_____

_____

_____

_____

_____

_____

_____

_____

_____

How have you seen this Wing enhance your
Main Type?

How does it impact your relationships, work, and
everyday life?

How does the other Wing influence your Main Type?

How can you utilize it more to create balance?

The Triads

The next set of directional signals we'll discuss are the Triads. We can group the nine personality Types in many ways, and the most common one is by groupings of three, or Triads. The three Types in each group share common assets and liabilities. For each person one Triad is more dominant (the one with your Main Type) than the other two.

Though we could name several different Triads within the Enneagram, the best known is the Center of Intelligence Triad:

- Feeling Center (Heart Triad): Types 2, 3, and 4
- Thinking Center (Head Triad): Types 5, 6, and 7
- Instinctive Center (Gut Triad): Types 8, 9, and 1

Two commonalities drive the Enneagram Types in each of these three centers: a common emotional imbalance and a common desire.

In the Heart Triad, Types 2, 3, and 4 are imbalanced in their *feelings*. This group shares similar assets and liabilities related to how they feel and engage in life through their feelings. Type 2s feel other people's emotions. Type 3s access their emotions the least, concerned that those emotions will hinder them from accomplishing tasks. Type 4s feel all their emotions with depth and intensity. All three Types react to their *emotional struggles* with *shame*.

Those in the Heart Triad focus on a desire for a *specific identity or significance* that they want others to recognize. Type 2s want to be seen as the most supportive, caring, and selfless person. Type 3s want to be seen as the most successful, admirable, and accomplished person. And Type 4s want to be seen as special, different, and unique.

When you are healthy as a Type 2, you are loving, compassionate, and generous. You have the amazing ability to sustain positive affections for others, going out of your way to support, help, and care for them.

However, when you begin to struggle, you try to maintain an image of being completely selfless by constantly doing "helpful" things, motivated by a longing for validation that you are wanted and loved by others.

You seek external validation to avoid your struggle with shameful feelings of being unwanted

ENNEAGRAM TYPE 2

At Their Best	At Their Worst
Loving	Intrusive
Compassionate	Martyr-Like
Adaptable	Indirect
Nurturing	Manipulative
Generous	Possessive
Supportive	Flatter
Hospitable	Needy
Tuned in to How People Feel	Overly Accommodating

or unloved. Convincing yourself that you do not have needs of your own and that you can fully focus on the needs of others, you overinvest in helping them to avoid painful feelings of rejection. You strive to emphasize your positive feelings and suppress your anger, frustration, and any hint of self-interest.

Going Deeper

What stands out to you about being in the Feeling Triad and your propensity for feelings of shame?

How attuned are you to your thinking and gut instincts in comparison to feelings?

In what ways do you wrestle with shame and try to serve others in order to avoid feeling rejected?

Do these efforts bring the love and closeness you wanted?

Where do your strengths of thoughtfulness, support, and nurture shine the most?

Childhood Message

Before we discuss the last set of directional signals (the Enneagram Paths), we need to understand what the Enneagram calls a Childhood Message.

From birth, everyone has a unique perspective on life, our personality Type's perspective. We all tend toward particular assumptions or concerns, and these develop into a Childhood Message. Our parents, teachers, and authority figures may have directly communicated this message to us, but most of the time, we interpreted what they said or did through the lens of our personality Type to fit this belief.

Sometimes we can see a direct correlation

between our Childhood Message and a childhood event; other times we can't. Somewhere, somehow, we picked up a message that rang true for us because of our personality Type's hardwiring. This false interpretation of our circumstances was and still is painful to us, profoundly impacting us as children and as adults.

Gaining insight into how our personality Type interpreted events and relationships in childhood will help us identify how that interpretation is impacting us today. Believing our Childhood Message causes our personality to reinforce its strategies to protect us from our Core Fear—apart from God's truth. Once we understand the message is hardwired into our thinking, we can experience God's healing truth and live more freely.

What's more, when we know the Childhood Message of others, we can begin to understand why they do what they do and how we can communicate with them more effectively.

As a Type 2, your Childhood Message is: "It's not okay to have your own needs."

The message your heart longed to hear as a child is your Core Longing: "You are wanted and loved."

·   ·   ·

Even as children, Type 2s were caring, kind, warm, and focused on pleasing others. They expressed themselves in loving and generous ways to earn attention, praise, and affection.

Another way they learned to earn love and affection was to use their superpower of intuitively knowing other people's emotions and needs. They had an uncanny ability to give others exactly what they need without being asked. As you can imagine, when people are given exactly what they need, they are surprised, delighted, and thankful.

Type 2 children became addicted to these reactions from others, so they began initiating this experience again and again. Whenever they could sense they were loved or wanted, they brought out this gift and (consciously or unconsciously) manipulated others into showing them the affection they craved.

Through their behavior Type 2 children were asking, "Do you love me now?" They read their parents' expressions and body language to assess whether they were loved or not, wanted or not, worthy or not. If they could not sense the love of their parents, they would feel deflated and hurt.

Type 2s do not see themselves as lovable, selfless, and kind. They are constantly stretching themselves to be kinder and more selfless to ensure that others will love and appreciate them.

Knowing your personality Type's Childhood Message will help you break free from childhood perceptions and reinterpret pieces of your story from a better vantage point. As you explore this, be gracious to yourself and your past. Be sensitive, nonjudgmental, caring, and kind to yourself. And remember, only God can fully redeem your past. He can free you from chains that bind, heal wounds that linger, and restore you to freedom.

Going Deeper

To what degree do you relate to the Type 2 Childhood Message?

What stories come to mind when you hear it?

What circumstances in the present have repeated this message from the past?

_____

_____

_____

_____

_____

_____

_____

What advice would you give to your childhood self in light of this message?

_____

_____

_____

_____

_____

_____

_____

Enneagram Paths

The final directional signals we'll discuss are the Enneagram Paths, which the inner lines and arrows in the Enneagram diagram display. The lines and arrows going out from our Main Type point to our Connecting Types. As a Type 2, you connect to Types 8 and 4.

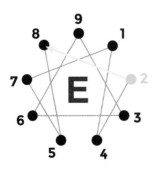 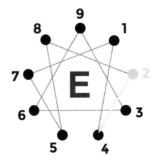

Remember, we can access both positive and negative characteristics of a Type we are connected to. The kind we access depends on whether we are aligned, misaligned, or out of alignment with God's truth.

Here is an overview of the four Enneagram Paths, which we'll discuss further in the following readings:

- *Stress Path*: When we're under stress, we tend to take on some of the misaligned or out-of-alignment characteristics of our Stress Path Type. For Type 2, these are the negative aspects of Type 8.
- *Blind Spot Path*: When we're around those we're most familiar with (mainly family), we display the misaligned characteristics of our Blind Spot Path Type. We typically do not see these characteristics in ourselves easily. For Type 2, these are the negative aspects of Type 4.
- *Growth Path*: When we believe and trust

that God loves us and that all He has is ours in Christ, we begin to move in a healthier direction, accessing the aligned characteristics of our Connecting Type. For Type 2, these are the positive aspects of Type 4.

- *Converging Path*: After making progress on the Growth path, we can reach the most aligned point of our Type, which is where three healthy Types come together. Here we access the healthiest qualities of our Main Type, our Growth Path's Type, and our Stress Path's Type.

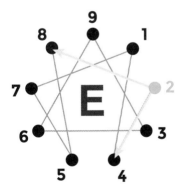

Going Deeper

In what direction is your heart currently heading?

_____

_____

_____

_____

_____

_____

_____

What concerns are you wrestling with?

_____

_____

_____

_____

_____

_____

_____

What growth have you experienced recently?

When you look at the four paths, what path have you been traveling recently? Why?

Stress Path

Under stress, you tend to move in the direction of the arrow below, taking on some of the misaligned characteristics of Type 8. Learning to identify these behavior patterns can serve as a rumble strip warning that you're veering off course. Then you can

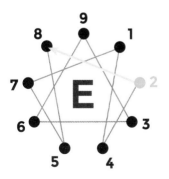

stop, pray for God's help, and move in a healthier direction for your personality.

As a Type 2 moving toward the average or unhealthy Type 8, you may:

- become irritable and defensive if you feel your love and support have been ignored or rejected.
- have controlling, aggressive, demanding, and dominating reactions toward others.
- become confrontational and angry.
- threaten to withdraw your support and care.
- manipulate others into doing what you want.
- blame problems on others, seeing issues as one-sided rather than owning any responsibility.

Going Deeper

Describe a stressful time when you took on some of these tendencies. What was the situation, and why were you triggered to respond this way?

When have you become irritable, defensive, controlling, and dominating and why?

What things in your life cause the most stress for you?

TYPE 2 UNDER STRESS

When under stress, **Type 2** will start to exhibit some of the average to unhealthy characteristics of **Type 8**.

Becoming egocentric, irritable, aggressive, and dominating

Becoming controlling of everyone and everything

Having outbursts of anger and aggressive confrontations, or threatening to withdraw their support from others

Blind Spot Path

When you're around people you're most familiar with—family members or close friends—you
express yourself more freely. You show them parts
of yourself you don't show anyone else, for better
or worse. When you're uninhibited and not at your
best, you display the negative qualities of your personality. On this Blind Spot Path, you access the
misaligned attributes of your Connecting Type,
which is Type 4.

You may be unaware that you're behaving differently with your family members or close friends
than you are with other people. Be sure to take
note of this path when you're trying to understand

yourself and your reactions, because it may surprise you. Working on these negative aspects can improve the relationship dynamics with those you're closest to.

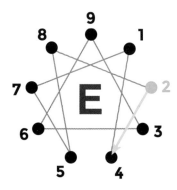

As a Type 2 moving toward the average or unhealthy Type 4, you may:

- openly share your feelings, needs, darker ambitions, and cravings.
- reveal hidden emotional and relational needs that go much deeper than others realize.
- express your disappointments in others.

- act in overly sensitive and emotional ways.
- become moody, temperamental, and self-absorbed.
- give yourself "treats" and become more self-indulgent.

Going Deeper

How do you respond when you feel overwhelmed in the presence of people you feel secure with versus those you're less comfortable with?

Which of the average or unhealthy tendencies do you resonate with the most?

Describe a situation where you reacted in the ways described above.

Growth Path

When you believe and trust that God loves you, and all He has is yours, you begin to relax and let go of your personality's constraints and lies. You draw nearer to Him and move in a direction that aligns you with His truth. You feel safe, secure, and loved.

Feeling more joy, peace, and liberation, you stretch yourself toward healthier attributes, even though it is hard. As you grow in faith and depend solely on Him, God blesses you with real and lasting transformation, shaping you into who He made you to be.

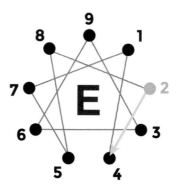

As a Type 2 moving toward the healthy side of Type 4, you can:

- become aware of your tendency to believe that you always have pure and unselfish motives.
- see your true heart, including unhealthy motives, and ask for forgiveness.
- take care of yourself and your own needs.
- discover your own emotions.
- accept painful feelings, including anger, sadness, and loneliness.
- believe that you are wanted and loved just as you are, apart from what you do for others.

Going Deeper

When you are growing, what changes about your heart and your typical responses?

Which of these growth attributes would you love to experience more in your life?

What helps to support your growth and flourishing?

How can you incorporate those things into your life more?

TYPE 2 DIRECTION OF **GROWTH**

When moving in the direction of growth, **Type 2** will start to exhibit some of the healthier characteristics of **Type 4**.

Becoming more self-nurturing and emotionally aware

Admitting and accepting painful feelings, including anger, sadness, and loneliness

Exploring their inner world; able to express themselves more creatively

Converging Path

You are your best self on the Converging Path, where three Types come together. Here you access the healthiest qualities of your Main Type, your Growth Path's Type, and your Stress Path's Type. When you live in the fullness of who you really are in Christ, you are freed from the bonds of your personality.

This path of personal transformation can be difficult to reach and maintain. When you first learn about the Converging Path, you may feel it's too hard to travel. But God wants to provide this path for you. Trust Him, follow Him, and ask Him to be with you as you move forward.

As a Type 2 moving toward the healthy side of Type 8, you may:

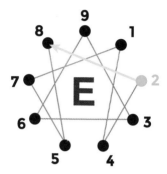

- own your strength and value apart from what others think.
- claim your positive and powerful presence by not solely focusing on others, but instead moving forward in God's calling and strength.
- express your irritations, hurt feelings, disappointments, and anger in a balanced way, not using passive-aggression or manipulation.
- shift your attention to what God thinks of you.
- become more independent and self-affirming.

Going Deeper

Can you recall a time when you experienced the freedom and joy of the Converging Path?

What was it like when you accessed the healthiest aspects of your Main Type, Growth Path's Type, and Stress Path's Type?

What would help you move toward your Converging Path more often?

Spiritual Renewal

TYPE 2
THE SUPPORTIVE ADVISOR

GOING DEEPER

Grab a journal and write down your physical, mental, and spiritual needs. Brainstorm a list of ways you could better care for yourself, or allow others to take care of you. Are there boundaries you need to draw or things you need to say "no" to? Reflect on the truth that you are loved by God, no matter how much you serve others or how much others appreciate you today.

Moving Toward Your Best Self

The journey of exploring your heart is not an easy one, but it's an exciting one.

God has a unique message for each Type. The message He tells you as a Type 2 is: "You are wanted and deeply loved."

When you were lost and far from Him, God knew your great need and sent His Son to rescue you. Christ showed His immense love for you by living a perfect life, dying on a cross for your sins, and rising from the dead to give you eternal life.

When you receive Christ as your Savior, He removes your sins and gives you His perfect righteousness, which brings immediate hope of a bright, freeing, and glorious future with Him. Trust in Him who loves you and went to such great lengths to meet your need.

After you place your trust in Him, you can completely rest in the assurance that you are wanted and loved perfectly. God cherishes you, provides for you, and pursues you. Knowing this allows you to loosen your grip on needing to be needed and receiving affection from others. It affirms your great value and worth, giving you freedom to acknowledge your own emotions and needs. From that position you can offer a humble, unselfish, and unconditional love for yourself and others.

Each Type has a signature Virtue, which you exhibit when you are at your best, and Type 2's Virtue is *humility*.

When you are truly humble, you are sincere, warmhearted, caring, and loving. With a generous spirit, you feel the needs of others intuitively. You interpret others' behavior charitably, emphasizing the good in people.

At your best, you do not need constant love and

affection from others for what you have done for them. You know that your worth comes from being a person God loves, and that your Good Shepherd takes care of your needs.

Using the Enneagram from a biblical perspective can empower you to see yourself with astonishing clarity so you can break free from self-condemnation, fear, and shame by experiencing unconditional love, forgiveness, and freedom. In Him, you are whole. And with Him by your side, you can grow stronger and healthier every day.

Now that you know how to use this internal GPS and its navigational signals, start using it every day. Tune in to how your heart is doing. Avoid your common pitfalls by staying alert to your rumble strips. As you learn new awareness and actions, you will move forward on the path that is healthiest for your personality Type and experience the gift of tremendous personal growth.

Going Deeper

What do you notice about yourself when you're at your best?

What would the world be like without the involvement of healthy Type 2s?

Type 2   VIRTUE

Humility is your virtue.

This gives you the ability to love
others without thoughts of self,
needing to be thanked, or even
repaid for what you gave from
the goodness of your heart.

What are some practical
ways you can offer your
virtue to others today?

Afterword

God's plan to restore the world involves all of us, which is why He made us so vastly different from each other in ways that reflect who He is.

That is why I'm so thrilled you picked up this book and have done the hard, but rewarding, work of looking into your heart. When you align with God's truth, you can support the kingdom, knit people together, and be the best *you* only you can be.

Growth is *not* easy. It requires us to surrender to God, depend on Him, and walk into His calling for us. But when we let go of our control and He takes over, He will satisfy our hearts, filling them with His goodness, and His blessings will flow into our lives and others' lives.

I can attest to God's transformative work having this ripple effect—reaching and positively impacting different parts of our lives and everyone we encounter. As I became more aligned with God's truth (and make no mistake, I'm still in progress!), the changes I was making helped transform my relationships with Jeff, my family, and other people around me. More and more friends, acquaintances, and even strangers were experiencing the transformation that comes from God through the tool of the Enneagram.

I can't wait to look back a year from now, five years from now, or even a decade from now, and hear about the ripple effects *your* transformation has created for hope, wholeness, and freedom. I'm excited about the path of discovery and growth ahead of you! What is God going to do in you with this new understanding of yourself and those around you? What are the things you'll hear Him whisper in your heart that will begin to set you free?

And how will your personal transformation bring positive change to the people in your life?

This is what I hope for you: First, that you will believe and trust in your identity in Christ. In Him, you are forgiven and set free. God delights in having you as His dear child and loves you unconditionally. This reality will radically change everything in you—it is the ultimate transformation from death to life.

Second, I hope that as you discover more about your Enneagram Type, you'll recognize how your personality apart from Christ is running *away* from your Core Fear, running *toward* your Core Desire, *stumbling* over your Core Weakness, and *desperate* to have your Core Longing met. As you become aware of these traits, you can make them the rumble strip alarms that point out what's going on in your heart. Then you can ask the Holy Spirit to help you navigate your inner world and refocus your efforts toward traveling the best path for your personality Type.

Third, I hope that God will reveal to you, both

in knowledge and experience, the transformative work of the Holy Spirit. With Him you can move toward growth, using all the tools of the Enneagram (the Levels of Alignment, the Wings, the Triads, the Enneagram Paths, etc.) to bring out the very best in you, the way God designed you to be. As a result, others will be blessed, God will be glorified, and you will experience the closeness of a Savior who will always meet your every longing and need.

May the love of Christ meet you where you are and pull you closer to God and others. And may you experience the joy of knowing His love for you in a deeper and more meaningful way.

Acknowledgments

My husband: I have to start by thanking my incredible husband, Jeff, who is my biggest cheerleader and supporter. He has helped me use the Enneagram from a biblical perspective and lovingly ensured that I expanded my gifts. Without his encouragement each step of the way, I never would have ventured into this world of writing. Thank you so much, Jeff.

My kids: Nathan and Libby McCord, you are a gift and blessing to me, and an inspiration for the work I do. Thank you for affirming me, being patient with me, and always believing in me. I pray this resource will bless you back as you journey through life.

My family: To my incredible parents, Dr. Bruce and Dana Pfuetze, who have always loved me well and encouraged me to move past difficulties by relying on the Lord. To my dear brother and sister-in-law, Dr. Mark and Mollie Pfuetze, thank you for being a source of support.

My team at Your Enneagram Coach: You enable me to be the best I can be as a leader, and I'm so honored to be a part of our amazing team. Thank you for letting me serve, for showing up every day, and for helping those who want to become more like Christ by using the Enneagram from a biblical perspective. Thank you, Danielle Smith, Traci Lucky, Robert Lewis, Lindsey Castleman, Justin Barbour, and Monica Snyder.

My marketing team, Well Refined Co.: Thank you, Christy Knutson, Jane Butler, JoAnna Brown, and Madison Church.

My agent: Thank you, Bryan Norman, for helping me navigate through all the ins and outs so that this could be the very best work for our readers. Your advice was most beneficial.

My publisher: To Adria Haley and the team at HarperCollins Christian, thank you for allowing me to share my passion for the Enneagram with the world in such a beautiful way through this book collection.

My writing team at StrategicBookCoach.com: Thank you, Danielle Smith, Karen Anderson, and Sharilyn Grayson for helping me create my manuscript.

My friend and advisor: Writing a book is harder than I expected and more rewarding than I could have ever imagined. None of this would have been possible without my most-cherished friend and beloved advisor, Karen Anderson. I am thankful for her heart, her passion, and her help every step of the way. You beautifully take my concepts and make them sing. Thank you!

About the Author

Beth McCord has been using the Enneagram in ministry since 2002 and is a Certified Enneagram Coach. She is the founder and Lead Content Creator of Your Enneagram Coach and cowrote *Becoming Us: Using the Enneagram to Create a Thriving Gospel-Centered Marriage* with her husband, Jeff. Beth has been featured as an Enneagram expert in magazines and podcasts and frequently speaks at live events. She and Jeff have two grown children, Nate and Libby, and live in Franklin, Tennessee, with their blue-eyed Australian Shepherd, Sky.

Continue Your Personal Growth Journey *Just for Type 2!*

Get your Type's in-depth online coaching course that is customized with guide sheets and other helpful insights so you can continue uncovering your personal roadmap to fast-track your growth, overcome obstacles, and live a more fulfilling life with God, others, and yourself.

The mission of YourEnneagramCoach.com is for people to see themselves with astonishing clarity so they can break free from self-condemnation, fear, and shame by knowing and experiencing unconditional love, forgiveness, and freedom in Christ.